*These notes refer to the Defamation Bill
as introduced in the House of Commons on 10 May 2012 [Bill 5]*

DEFAMATION BILL

EXPLANATORY NOTES

INTRODUCTION

1. These Explanatory Notes relate to the Defamation Bill as introduced in the House of Commons on 10 May 2012. They have been prepared by the Ministry of Justice in order to assist the reader of the Bill and to help inform debate. They do not form part of the Bill and have not been endorsed by Parliament.

2. The Notes are to be read in conjunction with the Bill. They are not, and are not meant to be, a comprehensive description of the Bill. Where a clause or part of a clause does not seem to require any explanation or comment, none is given.

SUMMARY

3. The Defamation Bill reforms aspects of the law of defamation. The civil law on defamation has developed through the common law over a number of years, periodically being supplemented by statute, most recently the Defamation Act 1952 ("the 1952 Act") and the Defamation Act 1996 ("the 1996 Act").

BACKGROUND

4. The Government's Coalition Agreement gave a commitment to review the law of defamation, and on 9 July 2010 the Government announced its intention to publish a draft Defamation Bill. The *Draft Defamation Bill* (Cm 8020) was published for full public consultation and pre-legislative scrutiny on 15 March 2011.

Bill 5—EN   55/2

These notes refer to the Defamation Bill
as introduced in the House of Commons on 10 May 2012 [Bill 5]

5. The public consultation closed on 10 June 2011. The Ministry of Justice received 129 responses from a range of interested parties. A comprehensive summary of the responses received was published on 24 November 2011 (*Draft Defamation Bill Summary of Responses to Consultation CP(R) 3/11*). In addition to the Government consultation, pre-legislative scrutiny of the draft Bill was undertaken by a Parliamentary Joint Committee. The committee held oral evidence sessions between April and July 2011 and its final report was published on 19 October 2011 (*The Joint Committee on the Draft Defamation Bill Report* Session 2010-2012, HL 203, HC 930-I).

6. The Government response to the Joint Committee's report was published on 29 February 2012 (*The Government's Response to the Report of the Joint Committee on the Draft Defamation Bill* Cm 8295*)* and set out the Government's conclusions including on certain matters raised in the public consultation but not specifically addressed in the Committee's report.

TERRITORIAL EXTENT AND APPLICATION

7. The Bill extends to England and Wales only.

8. In relation to Wales, the Bill does not relate to devolved matters or confer functions on the Welsh Ministers.

9. The Bill amends a number of enactments which extend to Scotland and Northern Ireland as well as to England and Wales. These amendments will extend to England and Wales only.

10. The Bill does not contain any provisions falling within the terms of the Sewel Convention. Because the Sewel Convention provides that Westminster will not normally legislate with regard to devolved matters in Scotland without the consent of the Scottish Parliament, if there are amendments relating to such matters which trigger the Convention, the consent of the Scottish Parliament will be sought for them.

COMMENTARY ON CLAUSES

Clause 1: Serious harm
11. This clause provides that a statement is not defamatory unless its publication has caused or is likely to cause serious harm to the reputation of the claimant. The provision extends to situations where publication is likely to cause serious harm in order to cover situations where the harm has not yet occurred at the time the action for defamation is commenced.

*These notes refer to the Defamation Bill
as introduced in the House of Commons on 10 May 2012 [Bill 5]*

12. The clause builds on the consideration given by the courts in a series of cases to the question of what is sufficient to establish that a statement is defamatory. A recent example is *Thornton v Telegraph Media Group Ltd*[1] in which a decision of the House of Lords in *Sim v Stretch*[2] was identified as authority for the existence of a "threshold of seriousness" in what is defamatory. There is also currently potential for trivial cases to be struck out on the basis that they are an abuse of process because so little is at stake. In *Jameel v Dow Jones & Co*[3] it was established that there needs to be a real and substantial tort. The clause raises the bar for bringing a claim so that only cases involving serious harm to the claimant's reputation can be brought.

Clause 2: Truth
13. This clause replaces the common law defence of justification with a new statutory defence of truth. The clause is intended broadly to reflect the current law while simplifying and clarifying certain elements.

14. *Subsection (1)* provides for the new defence to apply where the defendant can show that the imputation conveyed by the statement complained of is substantially true. This subsection reflects the current law as established in the case of *Chase v News Group Newspapers Ltd*[4], where the Court of Appeal indicated that in order for the defence of justification to be available "the defendant does not have to prove that every word he or she published was true. He or she has to establish the "essential" or "substantial" truth of the sting of the libel".

15. There is a long-standing common law rule that it is no defence to an action for defamation for the defendant to prove that he or she was only repeating what someone else had said (known as the "repetition rule"). Subsection (1) focuses on the imputation conveyed by the statement in order to incorporate this rule.

16. In any case where the defence of truth is raised, there will be two issues: i) what imputation (or imputations) are actually conveyed by the statement; and ii) whether the imputation (or imputations) conveyed are substantially true. The defence will apply where the imputation is one of fact.

17. *Subsections (2) and (3)* replace section 5 of the 1952 Act (the only significant element of the defence of justification which is currently in statute). Their effect is that where the statement complained of contains two or more distinct imputations, the defence does not fail if, having regard to the imputations which are shown to be substantially true, those which are not shown to be substantially true do not seriously harm the claimant's reputation. These provisions are intended to have the same effect as those in section 5 of the 1952 Act, but are expressed in more modern terminology.

---

[1] [2010] EWHC 1414.
[2] [1936] 2 All ER 1237.
[3] [2005] EWCA Civ 75.
[4] [2002] EWCA Civ 1772 at para 34.

The phrase "materially injure" used in the 1952 Act is replaced by "seriously harm" to ensure consistency with the test in clause 1 of the Bill.

18. *Subsection (4)* abolishes the common law defence of justification and repeals section 5 of the 1952 Act. This means that where a defendant wishes to rely on the new statutory defence the court would be required to apply the words used in the statute, not the current case law. In cases where uncertainty arises the current case law would constitute a helpful but not binding guide to interpreting how the new statutory defence should be applied.

Clause 3: Honest opinion
19. This clause replaces the common law defence of fair comment[5] with a new defence of honest opinion. The clause broadly reflects the current law while simplifying and clarifying certain elements, but does not include the current requirement for the opinion to be on a matter of public interest.

20. *Subsections (1) to (4)* provide for the defence to apply where the defendant can show that three conditions are met. These are condition 1: that the statement complained of was a statement of opinion; condition 2: that the statement complained of indicated, whether in general or specific terms, the basis of the opinion; and condition 3: that an honest person could have held the opinion on the basis of any fact which existed at the time the statement complained of was published or anything asserted to be a fact in a privileged statement published before the statement complained of.

21. Condition 1 (in *subsection (2)*) is intended to reflect the current law and embraces the requirement established in *Cheng v Tse Wai Chun Paul*[6] that the statement must be recognisable as comment as distinct from an imputation of fact. It is implicit in condition 1 that the assessment is on the basis of how the ordinary person would understand it. As an inference of fact is a form of opinion, this would be encompassed by the defence.

22. Condition 2 (in *subsection (3)*), reflects the test approved by the Supreme Court in *Joseph v Spiller*[7] that "the comment must explicitly or implicitly indicate, at least in general terms, the facts on which it is based". Condition 2 and Condition 3 (in *subsection (4)*) aim to simplify the law by providing a clear and straightforward test. This is intended to retain the broad principles of the current common law defence as to the necessary basis for the opinion expressed but avoid the complexities which have arisen in case law, in particular over the extent to which the opinion must be based on facts which are sufficiently true and as to the extent to which the statement must explicitly or implicitly indicate the facts on which the opinion is based. These

---

[5] Recently the Supreme Court in *Spiller v Joseph* [2010] UKSC 53 referred to this as honest comment.
[6] (2000) 10 BHRC 525.
[7] [2010] UKSC 53 (at para 105).

are areas where the common law has become increasingly complicated and technical, and where case law has sometimes struggled to articulate with clarity how the law should apply in particular circumstances. For example, the facts that may need to be demonstrated in relation to an article expressing an opinion on a political issue, comments made on a social network, a view about a contractual dispute, or a review of a restaurant or play will differ substantially.

23. Condition 3 is an objective test and consists of two elements. It is enough for one to be satisfied. The first is whether an honest person could have held the opinion on the basis of any fact which existed at the time the statement was published (in *subsection (4)(a)*). The subsection refers to "any fact" so that any relevant fact or facts will be enough. The existing case law on the sufficiency of the factual basis is covered by the requirement that "an honest person" must have been able to hold the opinion. If the fact was not a sufficient basis for the opinion, an honest person would not have been able to hold it.

24. The second element of condition 3 (in *subsection (4)(b)*) is whether an honest person could have formed the opinion on the basis of anything asserted to be a fact in a "privileged statement" which was published before the statement complained of. For this purpose, a statement is a "privileged statement" if the person responsible for its publication would have one of the defences listed in *subsection (7)* of the clause if an action was brought in respect of that statement. The defences listed are the defence of absolute privilege under section 14 of the 1996 Act; the defence of qualified privilege under section 15 of that Act; and the defences in clauses 4 and 6 of the Bill relating to responsible publication on a matter of public interest and peer-reviewed statements in a scientific or academic journal.

25. *Subsection (5)* provides for the defence to be defeated if the claimant shows that the defendant did not hold the opinion. This is a subjective test. This reflects the current law whereby the defence of fair comment will fail if the claimant can show that the statement was actuated by malice.

26. *Subsection (6)* makes provision for situations where the defendant is not the author of the statement (for example where an action is brought against a newspaper editor in respect of a comment piece rather than against the person who wrote it). In these circumstances the defence is defeated if the claimant can show that the defendant knew or ought to have known that the author did not hold the opinion.

27. *Subsection (8)* abolishes the common law defence of fair comment. This means that where a defendant wishes to rely on the new statutory defence of honest opinion the court would be required to apply the words used in the clause, not the current case law. In cases where uncertainty arises the case law would constitute a helpful but not binding guide to interpreting how the new defence should be applied.

28. *Subsection (8)* also repeals section 6 of the 1952 Act. Section 6 provides that in an action for libel or slander in respect of words consisting partly of allegations of

fact and partly of expression of opinion, a defence of fair comment shall not fail by reason only that the truth of every allegation of fact is not proved if the expression of opinion is fair comment having regard to such of the facts alleged or referred to in the words complained of as are proved. This provision is no longer necessary in light of the new approach set out in *subsection (4)*. A defendant will be able to show that conditions 1, 2 and 3 are met without needing to prove the truth of every single allegation of fact relevant to the statement complained of.

Clause 4: Responsible publication on matter of public interest
29. This clause creates a new defence to an action for defamation of responsible publication on a matter of public interest. It is based on the existing common law defence established in *Reynolds v Times Newspapers*[8] and is intended to reflect the principles established in that case and in subsequent case law. *Subsection (1)* provides for the defence to be available in circumstances where the defendant can show that the statement complained of was, or formed part of, a statement on a matter of public interest and that he or she acted responsibly in publishing the statement.

30. In relation to the first limb of this test, the clause does not attempt to define what is meant by "the public interest". However, this is a concept which is well-established in the English common law. It is made clear that the defence applies if the statement complained of "was, *or formed part of*, a statement on a matter of public interest" to ensure that either the words complained of may be on a matter of public interest, or that a holistic view may be taken of the statement in the wider context of the document, article etc in which it is contained in order to decide if overall this is on a matter of public interest.

31. In relation to the second limb, *subsection (2)* sets out a non-exhaustive list of matters to which the court may have regard in determining whether a defendant acted responsibly in publishing a statement. These are broadly based on the factors established by the House of Lords in *Reynolds* and subsequent case law[9]. However, the clause seeks to address particular problems such as lack of clarity as to the scope of the defence. For example, reference is included at *subsection (2)(a)* to "the nature of the publication and its context" to reflect the flexible way in which the clause is to be applied and the need to bear in mind the circumstances in which the publisher was operating and the resources available to it (e.g. the context of a national newspaper is likely to be different from the context of a non-governmental organisation or scientific journal).

32. The factors listed at *subsection (2)* are not intended to operate as a checklist or set of hurdles for defendants to overcome, and the draft Bill adopts the approach of setting them out in an illustrative and non-exhaustive way for the courts to consider as

---

[8] [2001] 2 AC 127.
[9] In particular, *Jameel v Wall Street Journal* [2006] UKHL 44.

appropriate within the overall circumstances of each case and the context of the publication as a whole.

33. The second limb of the test does not require the court to determine whether it would have acted in the same way as the defendant. Instead, the second limb of the test merely requires the court to determine if the defendant "acted responsibly". This means that an allowance will be made for what has sometimes been referred to in the case law as "editorial discretion".

34. *Subsections (3)* and *(4)* are intended to encapsulate the core of the common law doctrine of "reportage" (which has been described by the courts as "a convenient word to describe the neutral reporting of attributed allegations rather than their adoption by the newspaper"[10]). In instances where this doctrine applies, the defendant does not need to have verified the information reported before publication because the way that the report is presented gives a balanced picture.

35. Accordingly, *subsection (3)* applies *subsection (4)* to those circumstances in which the publication was of an accurate and impartial account of a dispute between the claimant and some other party. In determining whether the defendant acted responsibly for the purposes of the section, the court should disregard any failure on the part of a defendant to seek to verify the truth of the imputation conveyed by the publication (which would naturally include any failure of the defendant to seek the claimant's views on the statement). This means that a defendant newspaper for example would not be prejudiced for a failure to verify where *subsection (4)* applies.

36. *Subsection (5)* makes clear for the avoidance of doubt that the defence provided by this clause may be relied on irrespective of whether the statement complained of is one of fact or opinion.

37. *Subsection (6)* abolishes the common law defence known as the Reynolds defence. This is because the statutory defence is intended essentially to codify the common law defence. While abolishing the common law defence means that the courts would be required to apply the words used in the statute, the current case law would constitute a helpful (albeit not binding) guide to interpreting how the new statutory defence should be applied. It is expected the courts would take the existing case law into consideration where appropriate.

Clause 5: Operators of websites
38. This clause creates a new defence for the operators of websites where a defamation action is brought against them in respect of a statement posted on the website.

---

[10] Per Simon Brown in *Al-Fagih* [2001] EWCA Civ 1634.

39. *Subsection (2)* provides for the defence to apply if the operator can show that they did not post the statement on the website. *Subsection (3)* provides for the defence to be defeated if the claimant can show that it was not possible for him or her to identify the person who posted the statement; that they gave the operator a notice of complaint in relation to the statement; and that the operator failed to respond to that notice in accordance with provisions contained in regulations to be made by the Secretary of State.

40. *Subsection (4)* sets out certain specific information which must be included in a notice of complaint. The notice must specify the complainant's name, set out the statement concerned and where on the website the statement was posted and explain why it is defamatory of the complainant. Regulations may specify what other information would need to be included in a notice of complaint.

41. *Subsection (5)* provides details in general terms of other provisions that may be included in regulations. These include provisions as to the action which an operator must take in response to a notice (which in particular may include action relating to the identity or contact details of the person who posted the statement and action relating to the removal of the post); provisions specifying a time limit for the taking of any such action and for conferring a discretion on the court to treat action taken after the expiry of a time limit as having been taken before that expiry. This would allow for provision to be made enabling a court to waive or retrospectively extend a time limit as appropriate.

42. *Subsection (5) and subsection (6)* enable, respectively, the making of other provision for the purposes of the section, and the making of different provision for different circumstances.

Clause 6: Peer-reviewed statement in scientific or academic journal etc
43. This clause creates a new defence of qualified privilege relating to peer-reviewed material in scientific or academic journals. The term "scientific journal" would include medical journals.

44. *Subsection (1) to (3)* provide for the defence to apply where two conditions are met. These are condition 1: that the statement relates to a scientific or academic matter; and condition 2: that before the statement was published in the journal an independent review of the statement's scientific or academic merit was carried out by the editor of the journal and one or more persons with expertise in the scientific or academic matter concerned. The requirements in condition 2 are intended to reflect the core aspects of a responsible peer-review process. *Subsection (8)* provides that the reference to "the editor of the journal" is to be read, in the case of a journal with more than one editor, as a reference to the editor or editors who were responsible for deciding to publish the statement concerned. This may be relevant where a board of editors is responsible for decision-making.

45. *Subsection (4)* extends the protection offered by the defence to publications in

the same journal of any assessment of the scientific or academic merit of a peer-reviewed statement, provided the assessment was written by one or more of the persons who carried out the independent review of the statement, and the assessment was written in the course of that review. This is intended to ensure that the privilege is available not only to the author of the peer-reviewed statement, but also to those who have conducted the independent review who will need to assess, for example, the papers originally submitted by the author and may need to comment.

46. *Subsection (5)* provides that the privilege given by the clause to peer-reviewed statements and related assessments also extends to the publication of a fair and accurate copy of, extract from or summary of the statement or assessment concerned.

47. By *subsection (6)* the privilege given by the clause is lost if the publication is shown to be made with malice which reflects the condition attaching to other forms of qualified privilege. *Subsection (7)(b))* has been included to ensure that the new clause is not read as preventing a person who publishes a statement in a scientific or academic journal from relying on other forms of privilege, such as the privilege conferred under clause 7(9) to fair and accurate reports etc of proceedings at a scientific or academic conference.

Clause 7: Reports etc protected by privilege
48. This clause amends the provisions contained in the 1996 Act relating to the defences of absolute and qualified privilege to extend the circumstances in which these defences can be used.

49. *Subsection (1)* replaces subsection (3) of section 14 of the 1996 Act, which concerns the absolute privilege applying to fair and accurate contemporaneous reports of court proceedings. Subsection (3) of section 14 currently provides for absolute privilege to apply to fair and accurate reports of proceedings in public before any court in the UK; the European Court of Justice or any court attached to that court; the European Court of Human Rights; and any international criminal tribunal established by the Security Council of the United Nations or by an international agreement to which the UK is a party. *Subsection (1)* replaces this with a new subsection, which extends the scope of the defence so that it also covers proceedings in any court established under the law of a country or territory outside the United Kingdom, and any international court or tribunal established by the Security Council of the United Nations or by an international agreement.

50. *Subsection (2)* amends section 15(3) of the 1996 Act by substituting the phrase "public interest" for "public concern", so that the subsection reads "This section does not apply to the publication to the public, or a section of the public, of matter which is not of public interest and the publication of which is not for the public benefit". This is intended to prevent any confusion arising from the use of two different terms with equivalent meaning in the Bill and in the 1996 Act. *Subsection (6)(b)* makes the same amendment to paragraph 12(2) of Schedule 1 to the 1996 Act in relation to the

privilege extended to fair and accurate reports etc of public meetings.

51. *Subsections (3)* to *(10)* make amendments to Part 2 of Schedule 1 to the 1996 Act in a number of areas so as to extend the circumstances in which the defence of qualified privilege is available. Section 15 of and Schedule 1 to the 1996 Act currently provide for qualified privilege to apply to various types of report or statement, provided the report or statement is fair and accurate, on a matter of public concern, and that publication is for the public benefit and made without malice. Part 1 of Schedule 1 sets out categories of publication which attract qualified privilege without explanation or contradiction. These include fair and accurate reports of proceedings in public, anywhere in the world, of legislatures (both national and local), courts, public inquiries, and international organisations or conferences, and documents, notices and other matter published by these bodies.

52. Part 2 of Schedule 1 sets out categories of publication which have the protection of qualified privilege unless the publisher refuses or neglects to publish, in a suitable manner, a reasonable letter or statement by way of explanation or correction when requested to do so. These include copies of or extracts from information for the public published by government or authorities performing governmental functions (such as the police) or by courts; reports of proceedings at a range of public meetings (e.g. of local authorities) general meetings of UK public companies; and reports of findings or decisions by a range of associations formed in the UK or the European Union (such as associations relating to art, science, religion or learning, trade associations, sports associations and charitable associations).

53. In addition to the protection already offered to fair and accurate copies of or extracts from the different types of publication to which the defence is extended, amendments are made by *subsections (4), (7)(b)* and *(10)* of the clause to extend the scope of qualified privilege to cover fair and accurate summaries of the material. For example, *subsection (4)* extends the defence to summaries of notices or other matter issued for the information of the public by a number of governmental bodies, and to summaries of documents made available by the courts.

54. Currently qualified privilege under Part 1 of Schedule 1 extends to fair and accurate reports of proceedings in public of a legislature; before a court; and in a number of other forums anywhere in the world. However, qualified privilege under Part 2 only applies to publications arising in the UK and EU member states. *Subsections (4), (6)(a), (7),* and *(8)* extend the scope of the defence to cover the different types of publication to which the defence extends anywhere in the world. For example, *subsection (6)* does this for reports of proceedings at public meetings, and *subsection (8)* for reports of certain kinds of associations.

55. *Subsection (5)* provides for qualified privilege to extend to a fair and accurate report of proceedings at a press conference held anywhere in the world for the

discussion of a matter of public interest. Under the current law as articulated in the case of *McCartan Turkington Breen v Times Newspapers Ltd*[11], it appears that a press conference would fall within the scope of a "public meeting" under paragraph 12 of Schedule 1 to the 1996 Act. This provision has been included in the Bill to clarify the position.

56. Currently Part 2 qualified privilege extends only to fair and accurate reports of proceedings at general meetings and documents circulated by UK public companies (paragraph 13). *Subsection (7)* of the clause extends this to reports relating to public companies elsewhere in the world. It achieves this by extending the provision to "listed companies" within the meaning of Part 12 of the Corporation Tax Act 2009 with a view to ensuring that broadly the same types of companies are covered by the provision in the UK and abroad.

57. *Subsection (9)* inserts a new paragraph into Schedule 1 to the 1996 Act to extend Part 2 qualified privilege to fair and accurate reports of proceedings of a scientific or academic conference, and to copies, extracts and summaries of matter published by such conferences. It is possible in certain circumstances that Part 2 qualified privilege may already apply to academic and scientific conferences (either where they fall within the description of a public meeting in paragraph 12, or where findings or decisions are published by a scientific or academic association (paragraph 14)). The amendments made by *subsection (9)* of the clause will however ensure that there is not a gap.

58. *Subsection (11)* substitutes new general provisions in Schedule 1 to reflect the changes that have been made to the substance of the Schedule. It also removes provisions allowing for orders to be made by the Lord Chancellor identifying "corresponding proceedings" for the purposes of paragraph 11(3) of the Schedule, and "corresponding meetings and documents" for the purposes of paragraph 13(5). The provision relating to paragraph 13(5) no longer has any application in the light of the amendments made to that paragraph by *subsection (7)*, while the power in relation to paragraph 11(3) has never been exercised and the amendment leaves the provision to take its natural meaning.

Clause 8: Single publication rule
59. This clause introduces a single publication rule to prevent an action being brought in relation to publication of the same material by the same publisher after a one year limitation period from the date of the first publication of that material to the public or a section of the public. This replaces the longstanding principle that each publication of defamatory material gives rise to a separate cause of action which is subject to its own limitation period (the "multiple publication rule").

---

[11] [2001] 2 AC 277.

60. *Subsection (1)* indicates that the provisions apply where a person publishes a statement to the public (defined in *subsection (2)* as including publication to a section of the public), and subsequently publishes that statement or a statement which is substantially the same. The aim is to ensure that the provisions catch publications which have the same content or content which has changed very little so that the essence of the defamatory statement is not substantially different from that contained in the earlier publication. Publication to the public has been selected as the trigger point because it is from this point on that problems are generally encountered with internet publications and in order to stop the new provision catching limited publications leading up to publication to the public at large. The definition in *subsection (2)* is intended to ensure that publications to a limited number of people are covered (for example where a blog has a small group of subscribers or followers).

61. *Subsection (3)* has the effect of ensuring that the limitation period in relation to any cause of action brought in respect of a subsequent publication within scope of the clause is treated as having started to run on the date of the first publication.

62. *Subsection (4)* provides that the single publication rule does not apply where the manner of the subsequent publication of the statement is "materially different" from the manner of the first publication. *Subsection (5)* provides that in deciding this issue the matters to which the court may have regard include the level of prominence given to the statement and the extent of the subsequent publication. A possible example of this could be where a story has first appeared relatively obscurely in a section of a website where several clicks need to be gone through to access it, but has subsequently been promoted to a position where it can be directly accessed from the home page of the site, thereby increasing considerably the number of hits it receives.

63. *Subsection (6)* confirms that the section does not affect the court's discretion under section 32A of the Limitation Act 1980 to allow a defamation action to proceed outside the one year limitation period where it is equitable to do so. It also ensures that the reference in subsection (1)(a) of section 32A to the operation of section 4A of the 1980 Act (section 4A concerns the time limit applicable for defamation actions) is interpreted as a reference to the operation of section 4A together with clause 8. Section 32A provides a broad discretion which requires the court to have regard to all the circumstances of the case, and it is envisaged that this will provide a safeguard against injustice in relation to the application of any limitation issue arising under this clause.

Clause 9: Action against a person not domiciled in the UK or a Member State etc
64. This clause aims to address the issue of "libel tourism" (a term which is used to apply where cases with a tenuous link to England and Wales are brought in this jurisdiction). *Subsection (1)* focuses the provision on cases where an action is brought against a person who is not domiciled in the UK, an EU Member State or a state which is a party to the Lugano Convention. This is in order to avoid conflict with European jurisdictional rules (in particular the Brussels Regulation on jurisdictional

matters[12]).

65. *Subsection (2)* provides that a court does not have jurisdiction to hear and determine an action to which the clause applies unless it is satisfied that, of all the places in which the statement complained of has been published, England and Wales is clearly the most appropriate place in which to bring an action in respect of the statement. This means that in cases where a statement has been published in this jurisdiction and also abroad the court will be required to consider the overall global picture to consider where it would be most appropriate for a claim to be heard. It is intended that this will overcome the problem of courts readily accepting jurisdiction simply because a claimant frames their claim so as to focus on damage which has occurred in this jurisdiction only. This would mean that, for example, if a statement was published 100,000 times in Australia and only 5,000 times in England that would be a good basis on which to conclude that the most appropriate jurisdiction in which to bring an action in respect of the statement was Australia rather than England. There will however be a range of factors to take into account including, for example, whether there is reason to think that the claimant would not receive a fair hearing elsewhere. The Civil Procedure Rule Committee will be asked to consider including relevant factors in the Civil Procedure Rules.

66. *Subsection (3)* provides that the references in *subsection (2)* to the statement complained of include references to any statement which conveys the same, or substantially the same, imputation as the statement complained of. This addresses the situation where a statement is published in a number of countries but is not exactly the same in all of them, and will ensure that a court is not impeded in deciding whether England and Wales is the most appropriate place to bring the claim by arguments that statements elsewhere should be regarded as different publications even when they are substantially the same.

67. It is the intention that this new rule will be capable of being applied within the existing procedural framework for defamation claims. For example, if a person applied under CPR rule 6.36 for permission to serve a claim form out of the jurisdiction, the court would refuse to exercise its discretion to grant permission if it thought that it would not have jurisdiction to hear the claim as a result of this clause. If permission to serve a claim form out of the jurisdiction was granted under rule 6.36 and the claim form was served, it would be open to the defendant to make an application under CPR rule 11(1)(a) disputing the court's jurisdiction relying on this clause; and the court, if satisfied that it has no jurisdiction to hear the claim, would make an order to set aside the claim form and service of it.

Clause 10: Action against a person who was not the author, editor etc

---

[12] Council Regulation (EC) 44/2001 on jurisdiction and the recognition and enforcement of judgments in civil and commercial matters.

68. This clause limits the circumstances in which an action for defamation can be brought against someone who is not the primary publisher of an allegedly defamatory statement.

69. Subsection (1) provides that a court does not have jurisdiction to hear and determine an action for defamation brought against a person who was not the author, editor or publisher of the statement complained of unless it is satisfied that it is not reasonably practicable for an action to be brought against the author, editor or publisher.

70. Subsection (2) confirms that the terms "author", "editor" and "publisher" are to have the same meaning as in section 1 of the 1996 Act. By subsection (2) of that Act, "author" means the originator of the statement, but does not include a person who did not intend that his statement be published at all; "editor" means a person having editorial or equivalent responsibility for the content of the statement or the decision to publish it; and "publisher" means a commercial publisher, that is, a person whose business is issuing material to the public, or a section of the public, who issues material containing the statement in the course of that business. Examples of persons who are not to be considered the author, editor or publisher are contained in subsection (3) of section 1 of the 1996 Act.

Clause 11: Trial to be without a jury unless the court orders otherwise
71. This clause removes the presumption in favour of jury trial in defamation cases.

72. Currently section 69 of the Senior Courts Act 1981 and section 66 of the County Courts Act 1984 provide for a right to trial with a jury in certain civil proceedings (namely malicious prosecution, false imprisonment, fraud, libel and slander) on the application of any party, "unless the court considers that the trial requires any prolonged examination of documents or accounts or any scientific or local investigation which cannot conveniently be made with a jury".

73. *Subsection (1)* and *subsection (2)* respectively amend the 1981 and 1984 Acts to remove libel and slander from the list of proceedings where a right to jury trial exists. The result will be that defamation cases will be tried without a jury unless a court orders otherwise.

Clause 12: Power of court to order a summary of its judgment to be published
74. In summary disposal proceedings under section 8 of the 1996 Act the court has power to order an unsuccessful defendant to publish a summary of its judgment where the parties cannot agree the content of any correction or apology. Clause 12 gives the court power to order a summary of its judgment to be published in defamation proceedings more generally.

75. *Subsection (1)* enables the court when giving judgment for the claimant in a defamation action to order the defendant to publish a summary of the judgment.

Subsections (2) provides that the wording of any summary and the time, manner, form and place of its publication are matters for the parties to agree. Where the parties are unable to agree, *subsections (3)* and *(4)* respectively provide for the court to settle the wording, and enable it to give such directions in relation to the time, manner, form or place of publication as it considers reasonable and practicable. *Subsection (5)* disapplies the clause where the court gives judgment for the claimant under section 8(3) of the 1996 Act. The summary disposal procedure is a separate procedure which can continue to be used where this is appropriate.

Clause 13: Actions for slander: special damage
76. This clause repeals the Slander of Women Act 1891 and overturns a common law rule relating to special damage.

77. In relation to slander, some special damage must be proved to flow from the statement complained of unless the publication falls into certain specific categories. These include a provision in the 1891 Act which provides that "words spoken and published...which impute unchastity or adultery to any woman or girl shall not require special damage to render them actionable". *Subsection (1)* repeals the Act, so that these circumstances are not exempted from the requirement for special damage.

78. *Subsection (2)* abolishes the common law rule which provides an exemption from the requirement for special damage where the imputation conveyed by the statement complained of is that the claimant has a contagious or infectious disease. In case law dating from the nineteenth century and earlier, the exemption has been held to apply in the case of imputations of leprosy, venereal disease and the plague.

Clause 14: Meaning of "publish" and "statement"
79. This clause sets out definitions of the terms "publish", "publication" and "statement" for the purposes of the Bill. Broad definitions are used to ensure that the provisions of the Bill cover a wide range of publications in any medium, reflecting the current law.

Clause 15: Consequential amendments and savings etc
80. *Subsections (1) to (3)* make consequential amendments to section 8 of the Rehabilitation of Offenders Act 1974 to reflect the new defences of truth and honest opinion. Section 8 of the 1974 Act applies to actions for libel or slander brought by a rehabilitated person based on statements made about offences which were the subject of a spent conviction.

81. *Subsections (4) to (8)* contain savings and interpretative provisions.

FINANCIAL EFFECTS OF THE BILL

82. Implementation of the provisions of the Bill is not expected to impose any significant additional burden on the Consolidated Fund or the National Loans Fund or

to increase significantly any other public expenditure.

EFFECTS OF THE BILL ON PUBLIC SECTOR MANPOWER

83. No significant change in the workload of any Government department or agency is anticipated on implementation of this Bill.

SUMMARY OF THE IMPACT ASSESSMENT

84. The Impact Assessment (available at www.ialibrary.bis.gov.uk) analyses the costs and benefits of implementing the proposals included in the Bill. It has not been possible to quantify the majority of the identified impacts, and instead a qualitative assessment has been made.

85. Businesses may be claimants or defendants in defamation proceedings, and in particular website operators are likely to be businesses. Overall, we expect the package of proposals to reduce costs to business. However, due to significant uncertainty, on a conservative basis we have assessed the impact of the proposals as neutral for business.

86. An equality impact assessment initial screening has also been completed and concluded that there will not be any significant equality impacts as a result of these measures.

COMPATIBILITY WITH THE EUROPEAN CONVENTION ON HUMAN RIGHTS

87. Section 19 of the Human Rights Act 1998 requires the Minister in charge of a Bill in either House of Parliament to make a statement before Second Reading about the compatibility of the provisions of the Bill with the Convention rights (as defined by section 1 of that Act). The Secretary of State for Justice, Kenneth Clarke, has made the following statement:

"In my view the provisions of the Defamation Bill are compatible with the Convention rights."

88. There are several aspects of the Convention which are relevant to the provisions in this Bill, most notably Article 10 and Article 8.

89. Article 10(1) protects the right to freedom of expression. Subject to Article 10(2), it is "applicable not only to "ideas" and "information" that are favourably

received or regarded as inoffensive... but also to those that offend, shock or disturb."[13] The right is qualified by the exceptions and limitations contained in Article 10(2). Accordingly, its exercise may be subject to restrictions where necessary in a democratic society for the protection of the reputation of others.

90. Different forms of expression attract different levels of protection under the Convention. For example, political speech is of the "highest importance" and "restrictions on this freedom need to be examined rigorously by all concerned."[14]

91. The courts have recognised that reputation is a right which, as an aspect of private life, is protected by Article 8[15]. There remains debate about the extent to which Article 8 always includes a right to reputation (see, for example, *Karako v Hungary*[16]).

92. Given that this Bill will apply in a very wide range of contexts, the Government has proceeded on the basis that a fair balance needs to be struck in law between both Article 10 and Article 8 rights. In *Von Hannover v Germany*[17] the European Court of Human Rights held there is a need to ensure such a balance where both Articles 8 and 10 are engaged.[18]

93. The Government considers this Bill strikes the right balance, and, as appropriate, gives due flexibility for courts, when considering cases, to ensure that Convention rights are respected according to the extent to which the relevant rights are in play. The Notes that follow refer to particular issues that may be raised.

94. Clause 1 builds on existing case law and raises the bar for bringing a claim so that only cases involving serious harm to the claimant's reputation can be brought. The courts have recognised that a threat to a person's integrity under Article 8 must attain "a certain level of seriousness" or gravity[19]. The Government considers the test strikes a fair and proportionate balance. When judged in the balance with the right to freedom of expression, if the claimant cannot show he has been seriously harmed by publication of a statement, it is appropriate that no action should flow.

95. Clause 3 broadly reflects the common law defence of fair comment (described as "one of the fundamental rights of free speech"[20]) but does not include the

---

[13] *Lingens v Austria*, (Application No. 9815/82) (at para 41).

[14] Lord Nicholls in *R v BBC, ex p Pro-Life Alliance* [2003] UKHL 23 (at para 6). See also *Lingens v Austria* (at para 42).

[15] *Cumpana and Mazare v Romania* (2004) 41 EHRR 29; *Re Guardian News Media Ltd and others* [2010] UKSC 1.

[16] Application no 39311/05.

[17] (2005) 40 EHRR 1.

[18] In *re Guardian News Media Ltd* at [43] the Supreme Court restates the well established principle that where both Articles 8 and 10 are in play the court must weigh the competing rights.

[19] *Wood v Commissioner for Police* [2009] EWCA Civ 414 at [22]; see also *A v Norway (Application no. 28070/06)*.

[20] Per Scott LJ in *Lyon v The Daily Delegraph Ltd* [1943] 1 KB 746.

requirement for the opinion to be on a matter of public interest. Under existing law, the public interest in fair comment has been interpreted broadly: it should not be confined "within narrow limits"[21]; it has "greatly widened"[22]. Indeed, in *Spiller,* Lord Phillips observed recently that there may be a case for widening the scope of the defence by removing the public interest requirement[23]. There was broad support for such a change on consultation and in the report of the Joint Committee on the Draft Defamation Bill ("the Joint Committee"). Taking into account those laws which protect the private rights of potential claimants (the tort of misuse of private information for example), the Government considers (and agrees with the Joint Committee in this regard) that the new law will offer the right balance between free speech on matters of honest opinion[24] and the right to reputation.

96. Clause 6 creates a new defence of qualified privilege in relation to peer-reviewed material in scientific or academic journals. In principle, this may already be protected through other forms of privilege or through the *Reynolds* defence. For example, as Lord Hoffmann has said "...the defence is of course available to anyone who publishes material of public interest in any medium. The question in each case is whether the Defendant behaved fairly and responsibly in gathering and publishing the information."[25] The Government agreed with the Joint Committee that there is a strong public interest rationale for clearer protection of responsible scientific and academic debate. The clause by its nature concerns matters of public interest and builds in safeguards in that protection is available only where the relevant statement has followed an independent, peer-review, process and is lost if made with malice.

97. Clause 8 introduces a single publication rule limiting actions being brought in relation to publication of the same material by the same publisher after one year from the date of first publication. Limitation periods can engage Article 6 where incompatible with an effective right of access to the court. Equally "...they serve important purposes, namely to ensure legal certainty and finality... "[26]. The clause does not affect the right of a claimant to take action to vindicate his reputation. In any case, *subsection (6)* confirms that the court retains a discretion through s.32A of the Limitation Act 1980 to waive the limitation period if it would be equitable to allow an action to proceed.

98. Clause 10 limits the circumstances in which an action for defamation can be brought against a person who is not the primary publisher of an allegedly defamatory statement. It is clear that Article 6 embodies not just procedural guarantees of fairness but also the right of access to the court itself[27]. This may, however, be subject to

---

[21] Per Lord Denning MR in *London Artists v Littler* [1969 2 QB 375 (at 391).
[22] *Spiller v Joseph* [2010] UKSC 53 (at para 108).
[23] Para 113.
[24] The clause retains the common law rule that the statement indicate, in general or specific terms, the basis for the opinion (see *subsection (3))*.
[25] *Jameel v Wall Street Journal* [2006] UKHL 44 (at para 54).
[26] *Stubbings v UK* (1996) 23 EHRR 213.
[27] *Golder v UK* (1975) 1 EHRR 524.

limitation as a right of access "by its very nature calls for regulation by the State ... [which will] enjoy a certain margin of appreciation"[28]. It is also clear that Article 6 does not affect the democratic power of the state to determine the scope of an individual's civil rights[29]. To the extent Article 6 is engaged at all, nothing in the clause impairs the "very essence"[30] of a claimant's right to take action to protect his reputation. The clause applies only to those persons who are not the author, editor or publisher for the purposes of s.1 of the 1996 Act. In any case, the clause leaves discretion to the court to hear a case if it is not reasonably practicable for a defamation action to be taken against the author etc.

COMMENCEMENT

99. The savings related provisions in subsections (4) to (8) of clause 15 and clause 16 (short title, commencement and extent) come into force on the day on which the Act is passed. Otherwise, the Bill will come into force on such day as the Secretary of State may specify by order (clause 16(3)).

---

[28] *Fayed v UK* (1994) 18 EHRR 393 (at 65).
[29] *Matthews v Ministry of Defence (HL) [2003] 1 All ER 689 (at para 77)*
[30] *Fayed v UK.*

DEFAMATION BILL

EXPLANATORY NOTES

These notes refer to the Defamation Bill as introduced in the House of Commons on 10 May 2012 [Bill 5]

Ordered, by The House of Commons,
to be Printed, 10 *May* 2012.

© Parliamentary copyright House of Commons 2012
This publication may be reproduced under the terms of the Parliamentary Click-Use Licence, available online through The National Archives website at
www.nationalarchives.gov.uk/information-management/our-services/parliamentary-licence-information.htm
Enquiries to The National Archives, Kew, Richmond, Surrey, TW9 4DU;
email: psi@nationalarchives.gsi.gov.uk

PUBLISHED BY AUTHORITY OF THE HOUSE OF COMMONS
LONDON — THE STATIONERY OFFICE LIMITED
Printed in the United Kingdom by The Stationery Office Limited
£3.50

Bill 5—EN (20588) 55/2